SCHIRMER PERFORMANCE EDITIONS

HAL LEONARD PIANO LIBRARY

DEBUSSY
SUITE BERGAMASQUE

Prélude, Menuet, Clair de lune, Passepied

Edited and Recorded by Christopher Harding

On the cover:
The Artist's Garden in Giverny (1900)
by Claude Monet (1840–1926)

ISBN 978-1-4803-6905-4

G. SCHIRMER, *Inc.*

DISTRIBUTED BY

HAL•LEONARD®

Contact us:
Hal Leonard
7777 West Bluemound Road
Milwaukee, WI 53213
Email: info@halleonard.com

In Europe, contact:
Hal Leonard Europe Limited
42 Wigmore Street
Marylebone, London, W1U 2RN
Email: info@halleonardeurope.com

In Australia, contact:
Hal Leonard Australia Pty. Ltd.
4 Lentara Court
Cheltenham, Victoria, 3192 Australia
Email: info@halleonard.com.au

CONTENTS

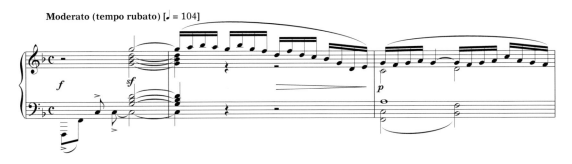

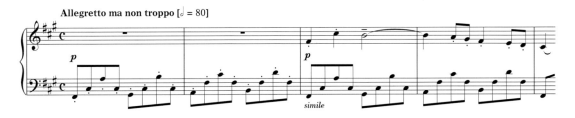

The price of this publication includes access to companion recorded performances online, for download or streaming, using the unique code found on the title page. Visit **www.halleonard.com/mylibrary** and enter the access code.

PERFORMANCE NOTES

Suite bergamasque, L. 75

The music we know as the *Suite bergamasque* had a somewhat awkward journey to its present form. Originally conceived and composed in 1890, the suite was bought for publication in 1891 but was never printed. It was not until 1905 (after changing hands a couple more times) that it was revised and published at a time in Debussy's life that saw him well established and indeed famous as a composer. His music was starting to be performed in concert often, and this addition to his published works capitalized on his popularity among cultivated (and practicing!) amateurs, as well as paid off a debt to a previous publisher.

"*Bergamasque*" is a term that refers to a dance from the region of Bergamo in Italy, a dance that was awkward and clownish in nature. Debussy chose aptly in using such an adjective for his suite, since the name functions evocatively on at least three levels:

First, it is an announcement that this is indeed a dance suite, albeit an atypical one (which is to say: non-German). Debussy the composer was intensely concerned with asserting French culture and musical history in the face of a dominating German ascendancy towards the end of the 19th and into the 20th centuries. Musically, a heavy "Wagnerism" dominated, and from the late 1880s, Debussy increasingly sought a way out from underneath its influence. *Suite bergamasque* hearkens back to the clavicinists of an earlier France, the famous composers and harpsichordists Louis and François Couperin, and Jean-Philipe Rameau, among others. The suite's movements are dances, but not arranged as we might find in suites by J.S. Bach or his German predecessors. Harmonic language, especially in the very forward-looking third movement, foreshadows the fully blossomed impressionism (so quintessentially French) that was finding utterance in Debussy's contemporary work around 1905: *L'isle joyeuse* (1904), *Estampes* (1903), and *La Mer* (for orchestra, 1905) to name but a few.

Second, "*bergamasque*" perhaps describes Debussy's own feelings regarding the music and pianism contained in the suite if we consider the term to be synonymous with "awkward," in line with the old prejudices. With the exception of "Clair de lune," the individual movements are indeed physically awkward to play, with much thought needing to be given to issues of *legato*, voicing, the sustain of certain notes in passages that require "creative" fingering, etc. They belong to an earlier style of pianistic writing for Debussy, one that thankfully seems to have been ironed out and more thoughtfully considered in his later compositions, especially from the turn of the century onwards.

Beyond this are the strange characteristics of several of the movements themselves: the menuet seems anything but the light, elegant, straightforward and simple dance we remember from the height of its social and musical supremacy during the time of Louis XIV, characteristics which were honored by seemingly all composers other than Debussy. Rather, its texture is thick (though it must sound transparent), its gestures awkward, its acrobatics more circus-like than court-like. Nor is this menuet content to exist within its traditional triple meter: it introduces several phrases of a distinct 4/4, although not written as such (mm. 5–8). "Clair de lune" (possibly originally titled "Promenade sentimentale") functions as a kind of sarabande, since it contains some rhythmic elements that we associate with that dance (the motion to the second beat, for instance, which dominates the opening section), but its very nature hearkens back to the original, rather more sensual character of the Spanish sarabandes before they were adopted and cleaned up by the French court. The passepied was originally titled a "Pavane," and is the only passepied in my experience that is in a duple meter, rather than a quick triple. There could be many reasons to speculate on the title change, but none assuage the fact that, as a passepied, this one is awkward to dance to.

Lastly, "*bergamasque*" serves as an evocation of the poem "Clair de lune" by the symbolist poet Paul Verlaine, the first lines of which are

Votre âme est un paysage choisi
Que vont charmant masques et bergamasques
Jouant du luth et dansant et quasi
Tristes sous leurs déguisements fantasques.

Your soul is a choice landscape
Wherein charming mimes and pantomimes
Are playing the lute and dancing and almost
Sad beneath their fantastic costumes.
                    (translation by Christopher Harding)

One of the main characteristics of symbolist poetry is the ambiguity, or multiplicity, of meaning in both choice of word and syntax. It makes translation imprecise and challenging, an opportunity to grasp at meaning and connotation rather than literal definition—a rather impressionistic task, if I may use that word. My translation in addition loses the beauty (and the meaning intrinsic to that beauty) of the original language; but here, of interest is the seeming duality of opposites in Verlain's choice of "*masques and bergamasques.*" Is one charming, and the other awkward? Are they both charming? The music of the *Suite bergamasque* is indeed uniformly charming, despite its "problems," pianistic and musical. I highly recommend that one search out Verlain's poem in its entirety, that more light be shed on Debussy's suite through personal interpretation and engagement with the poem's most beautiful text.

Debussy's Style in the *Suite bergamasque*

I have stated above that the *Suite bergamasque* is an early work, and only foreshadows the "Impressionism" of Debussy's more mature works. This suite does not exhibit the plethora of precise articulation markings, performance directions and descriptions that his later works do. In studying all of Debussy's music, however, our attention to detail and the interpretation of his markings must be as meticulous as when we approach the music of Haydn and Mozart. Debussy abhorred pianists who performed his music with cavalier freedom, expressing his desire on several occasions for a faithful interpreter, one who would not yield to the temptation of doing what is not written in the indulgence of "personal interpretation." It is true that we cannot and should not avoid real differences of performance expression among us, but we must strive to create in our minds an exact understanding of what is written.

An example of the questions raised by exact observation can be found on the first page of the Prélude of this suite. What is the difference between the *sforzando* marked on beat 3 of measure 1, and the "sideways accent" on beat 2 of measure 11? How are those sideways accents different from the *tenutos* found in m. 12, since an earlier composer like Schumann or Brahms would have used the accent sign to designate a *tenuto*? What is the difference between *cédez* (which means gradually slowing) and *ritardando* (also meaning a gradual slowing) when they are both used in immediate proximity in the same movement ("Passepied," mm. 80–87)? These questions should serve to make us decide exactly what is meant, and exactly how we want to perform.

This emphasis on the exact and the precise is very typical of the French aesthetic. It often manifests itself in a certain reserve or distance from its subject, eschewing emotional display, and seeks an elegant refinement of execution and effect. An exaggerated emotional expression most often destroys the natural beauty of gesture (musical or physical), a beauty that carries its own intrinsic emotional meaning. In the *Suite bergamasque*, Debussy has paid great attention to painting in music the gestures of dance, the arabesques of fancy, and the art of baroque intricacy. We ought not to overlay this with "emotionalism" beyond what is naturally expressed in the music itself.

German music is typically highly expressive, but French music is not—unless the composer explicitly asks for it, as does happen often enough (the tempo/character indication of "Clair de lune," for example). At such moments we must consider whether the *expressif* quality is best expressed through a choice of sound, the taking of time, or both; but it must be *thought* about and planned, especially by those of us who are not born and bred to the French aesthetic. We Americans tend to be impatient with the French world of elegant reserve, of subdued and refined emotion. Instead, we prefer to hold back very little in the name of "being real," pursuing straightforward and open honesty. Our culture is suspicious of reserve. But the beauty of entering into the music of another culture is the chance to grow in the understanding of our own, and to emerge as a greater human being. I don't believe that Debussy would call his music "reserved" in any way, but we might perceive it that way at first. The challenge is to understand and delight in its beauty on its own terms, to learn the lessons Debussy has to teach us, and not to appropriate the notes for our own purposes.

Sound, Color, and Pedal

Sound originates in the demands of our ear and imagination (by which I mean that we must have a precise idea of what kind of sound we want), but colors are produced from the fingertips by means of touch, through the use of the pedals, and through precise voicing. One of the most notable characteristics of Debussy's music is his use of many different layers of voicing and sound, very clearly sculpted and colored through a variety of touches, often within the same hand. But even this ought not to be exaggerated.

In seeking out a colorful voicing or balance among certain layers of sound, it is useful to play the various voices of a chord or passage with two hands before trying it with one hand. I feel it is important to get the sound in our ear first, by whatever means, before trying for its "proper" execution. If the ear demands it, the fingers and hands will find a way to produce it.

I also practice a lot without pedal, to hear the honest truth about what kind of sound, color, voicing and legato the fingers are (or are not) producing. Then the pedals ought to be added as enhancements. Of course, we use a lot of pedal for all sorts of purposes: harmonic, melodic, coloristic, etc. But pedaling should be finely coordinated with the work of the fingers as part of the overall sound, not as the producer of sound or color.

Debussy's approach to the keys was to be one with them—to be attached to them as extensions of our sensitive hands and fingers. This approach, combined with his famous admonition that the piano ought to be played as if it has no hammers, might lead us to conclude that he desired a "washy" or weakly articulated sound, but this is untrue. Even a cursory glance at any of his scores reveals a plethora of staccato notes and accents of various kinds. These must be respected and clearly articulated, while cultivating a very sensitive and sophisticated use of the pedals.

Debussy leaves us next to no explicit instruction in his scores of how he wanted us to use the pedals. There are some exceptions, but most often we are forced to resort to some sleuthing in order to figure out Debussy's intentions. Oftentimes Debussy will indicate his use of pedal by writing whole notes (especially in the bass) that can't be held with the fingers while we are playing in other registers of the piano with both hands. Sometimes pedaling can be used as a kind of "glue" for help in chord leaps or resolutions, frequent occurrences in the *Suite bergamasque*.

Debussy considered pedaling to be similar to breathing. I feel that the important thing about pedaling is not when to push it down, but rather when to release or change it, and how; this is much like swimmers, who have to be concerned with how they take breaths as they swim. Pedaling, whether using the damper pedal or the *una corda*, is perhaps the most individual of all things pianistic, and very difficult to notate and reproduce from pianist to pianist or from piano to piano. Pedaling is often used to color harmonies and melodies, and sometimes for rhythmic accentuation; but there are in addition to these uses many different levels of pedaling for both the damper and the *una corda* pedals. Sensitive pianists will find themselves using quarter, half, three-quarter and full pedals, sometimes barely touching the pedal, etc. All these uses and countless more are at our disposal, limited only by our imagination and penchant for exploration.

There are two crucial points about pedaling that should be made here. The first is very basic, but I see it in many advanced students and so I feel that I should make a statement about it: Pedaling is best accomplished with the ball of the foot (that fleshy area just behind the toes) resting firmly on the end of the pedal, with the heel on the floor. A great deal of sensitivity and "oneness" with the pedal is sacrificed when students pedal with the toes or with the instep of their foot.

Secondly, great attention should be paid to the "point of engagement" of the damper pedal. We should learn to listen for the point at which the dampers begin to damp the strings as we release the pedal. When we become sensitive to this moment in sound, we can begin to make use of the incredible subtleties to be had by very quick and shallow half and quarter pedal changes, hovering around the "point of engagement." I have found the following exercise to be useful. It is very much like learning to drive a manual transmission car, but mercifully without the danger of stalling out:

Play any note and depress the damper pedal to hold that note while you release the key. (One could do this in reverse order, but I like hearing the change in sound from the single set of strings vibrating to the entire set of piano strings vibrating in sympathy with the struck note.) Next, slowly release the pedal until you hear that the dampers have damped the strings completely, all the while noting the change of sound as the dampers come closer to the strings. At the point where the note stops ringing, cease to release the pedal. This is the "point of engagement," as I call it, the point where the dampers are completely touching the strings. Now, release the pedal entirely. Often we are surprised at the remaining distance and how far we have to press the pedal before the effect kicks in. The frustrating thing is that this distance is different on every piano.

Similar exercises can be developed for exploring the *una corda*—for instance, repeating a certain note with different depths of pedal. With sensitivity and knowledge of how these pedals can change the sound with subtle accuracy, we can make use of various depths of pedal for different sounds: full deep pedal for harmonic richness, shallow pedal for coloristic affects, etc. This is all dependent on the individual's ear, and a great deal of individual experimentation by teacher and student.

Pedaling does have a connection to dynamics. The damper pedal, in particular, produces a certain volume of sound that has to be dealt with if one is after an intimate effect; consider using less pedal in such a case. Sometimes it is acceptable to pedal through rests, because they are "articulation rests" which tell us to take the hand off the keyboard or to release a certain note for articulation purposes, not rests intended to produce silence. But other times we need to be careful to let rests speak clearly. Sometimes we must exaggerate our articulation in order to speak through the pedal. This is often the case when using the *una corda*, but also we must make sure to speak clearly with our fingers while using the damper pedal. Our fingers ought not to get weak simply because our foot is coming on strong. For instance, when I use the *una corda* in combination with a *decrescendo*, it is not as a substitute for doing the *decrescendo* with my fingers; it just helps to change the quality of the sound.

The range of dynamics in any given piece should be strictly observed and understood in their context. Dynamics are relative to one another and to the room in which we are playing, but they are also emotional, and indicative of feeling and expression. For example, a *mezzo forte* that occurs in a piece

which rarely rises above a *piano* is a dynamic of great importance. In the *Suite bergamasque*, we might be a little more direct in our dynamic range and changes than in Debussy's later works, but we must take care not to let our performance forsake the refinement of expression and self-control that is at once so very French and "very Debussy."

Fingering

The fingering contained herein are suggestions only. Fingerings vary according to the size and flexibility of different hands, and Debussy himself believed that fingerings were intensely personal. In the preface to his Études, he proclaims that in this matter one is never better served than by one's own self. But just as pedaling is useful for certain colors, so I find that certain fingerings encourage certain colors from my hand, and I use it to create a true *legato*. There are far fewer possibilities for fingerings than for pedaling, so I have offered some suggestions for those who might need some workable ideas.

Some of my ideas may come under the rubric "creative fingering." This is born out of my conviction that Debussy was indeed interested in a true finger *legato*, and notates his scores with that in mind, choosing carefully (I presume!) the rhythmic values of his notes. This leads to some very awkward and perplexing questions at times in the *Suite bergamasque*, especially in the opening two movements. At certain of those places I have explained in the following notes the kind of technique needed to execute my suggestions.

Notes On The Individual Movements

Prélude: Moderato (tempo rubato)

"To be played in a moderate tempo, with *rubato*." This flowing *tempo rubato* is to be understood as a flexible tempo, allowing for the relaxation of phrases at natural conclusions, as well as the forward momentum inspired by physical and musical gestures. Such *rubato* might be found both at the level of the phrase, and also at the level of individual rhythms, which need not be slavishly exact, but rather more natural in their speaking.

One can extend this flexibility to the matter of overall tempo relationships between sections of the piece's form (meaning that not every section need be exactly the same tempo). But one must at all times remember a basic pulse, so that every section belongs to the same organic piece, thereby avoiding any unnatural creations.

m. 1: An example of rhythmic *rubato* is found here in the opening measure: the second F on the "and" of beat 1 is released as the second note of a two-note slur, gently and unaccented. The C (to be played with RH) on beat 2 stands proudly on its own; the C on the "and" of beat 2 is a gestural pickup to the *sf* chord on beat 3. These rhythms all have different pronunciation, and should not be smoothed out in favor of the over-arching upward gesture, which is "so obvious a blind man could hear it." The G at the top of the right-hand chord must be played with a true *sf* (but within a dynamic that is *only* forte), supported by a firm knuckle and believing that it is part of the whole arm, not on its own. The inner voices of this chord can be played less, and in fact it is a good idea to practice playing the bass C and soprano G first, and adding the inside chord afterwards, softer, then playing as written with a voicing that has already been practiced (RH thumb not too loud). In this way, the G on top can ring with enough sound to carry through to the next measure as the true beginning of the phrase.

m. 2: The B-flat in the second group of sixteenth notes is indeed correct according to all the older editions I have seen. This measure and all similar ones can flow out of the hand very naturally with circular wrist motions.

m. 3: The downbeat (melody and LH chord) must resolve from the previous harmony. It is probably necessary to roll the left-hand chord, but it must be done subtly and swiftly. Because of the slur to the second left-hand chord, take care to leave room in the sound for that chord to resolve as well. Be sure to hold the A in the left-hand thumb for the full measure! Also in measure 4.

m. 4: The resolution on beat 3 is terribly beautiful indeed in the way it contrasts with the analogous place of the previous measure. However, since Debussy is precise in his layering of voices, be careful to keep each layer on its own level, and to make the listener clearly aware of what is color, and what is melody. In other words, be careful not to play the inner voices too loudly! The tied G both here and in measure 3 (as well as the tied F into m. 5) must be heard over the bottom voices.

m. 6: Note that the right-hand B-flat on beat 3 is held as a half note, in contrast to measure 71.

mm. 11 and similar: I have chosen this fingering because it respects Debussy's slurring, which, however, does not need to be as distinctly pronounced as one would in Mozart. Execute these double thirds with drops of the hands (from the wrist) on the "and" of beat three, and again on the "and" of beat 4.

mm. 12 and 14: Be sure to voice the top voice, so the melody stands out against the inner chords.

m. 15: This time, unlike measures 11 and 13, the C in the right-hand chord on the "and" of beat 1 should not be accented; it is *subito piano*. Crossing the second finger over the thumb on the final note provides a very nice release of the hand from the wrist, an instance of "physical and musical marriage," as it were. It also prepares the thumb for the next downbeat.

m. 19: Be sure that the *ritardando* which begins in measure 18 is continued all the way to end of measure 19. The pedaling for this measure is extremely difficult; it may have been possible on Debussy's piano to hold the damper pedal all the way through the measure (as seems indicated by the whole-note F in the bass) without too much blurring of the harmonies, but it seems impossible on modern instruments. A very gradual and subtle releasing of the damper pedal is required (1/4 pedal on the "and" of beat one, the "and" of beat 2, and again on beat 3?), which will lose the bass F only gradually and carefully.

mm. 20–44: In this section, it is important to feel the steady pulses of the tempo, in order to properly feel the syncopations of the melody. Still shape a long and flowing line, however, with appropriate relaxations at important harmonic moments.

m. 20: Although the thirty-second notes should sparkle, they should not be tossed off with no thought to clarity. (Even more so for the thirty-second notes in m. 22, which are more obviously melodic.) The right hand and left hand should be coordinated in such a way that the "flourish" in measure 20 is accomplished in one gesture.

m. 21: The left hand should release on beat 4 as the second note of the two-note slur. The right hand, however, continues on as one phrase.

m. 22: Be careful not to bang the end of the right-hand phrase on the "and" of beat 2, although it should sound well enough to be the true beginning of the following phrase.

m. 23: Note the difference between the last chord here (separate from the preceding phrase) and the last chord in measure 39 (tapered as the true end of the phrase).

m. 26: Despite the quick notes and the cross-hand technique (*m.g.* = *main gauche* = LH; *md* = *main droite* = RH), these notes must be as *legato* and well-shaped as possible, even from left hand to right hand. The left-hand chord on beat 3 will probably have to be rolled, but it should be subtle and soft, not sounding as part of the melody.

m. 30: The left-hand finger substitutions are precisely notated. I recommend not changing to the fourth finger until the tenor voice has completed its substitution from the second finger to the thumb.

m. 36: Note the *staccato* on the downbeat E in the soprano, which ought to be brightly articulated even if using pedal.

m. 49: I have put the option of using the second and fourth fingers on the "ands" of beats 1 and 2 because I enjoy the smoothing over of the sound on beats 2 and 3, as opposed to the heaviness of using the second and fourth fingers on those beats.

m. 51: Be sure to play the final right-hand C with enough sound so that it sets up a good, strong, **mf** dynamic, under which you can color and voice the following chords and *staccato* bells with spaciousness.

mm. 52–60: Each layer of sound should be different, each voice connecting linearly across the bar lines. *Staccatos* should be as sparks of light in a meteor shower.

mm. 60 and 62: A free arm behind your octaves will ensure a warm sound, as well as coordinating your arm movements with the left hand, which ought to create a *legato*-sounding line in one gesture.

mm. 61 and similar: there are many fingerings possible, and one doesn't have to hold the whole notes because of an extended pedal. But pay attention to the shape of Debussy's slurs here.

m. 65: Every note of the trill must shine!

mm. 74–75: As in measures 3–4, be sure to hold the alto Ds for the entire measure! But in this case, let go of them with the thumb after catching them with the pedal when changing on beat 3 of each measure.

mm. 76–77: Be careful not to *crescendo* too strongly here; there is more to come in measure 78. The pedal could be changed on each quarter beat, but subtly so as not to lose the bass C octave too soon.

m. 81: I choose this fingering again to respect Debussy's slurs. I would probably give in to holding the bass F octave in the pedal until the fourth beat, at which point I would change to emphasize the change of harmony and the start of the new slur.

m. 88: I would definitely hold the pedal throughout this measure, treating these rests as "articulation rests"—which means, release the hands, but not the sound. In light of the fact that I release beat one immediately in measure 89, I confess that I can't defend this practice logically, only artistically.

Menuet: Andantino; *pp* et très délicatement

m. 1: Do not miss the fact that dynamic and character indications are listed above the staff, along with tempo: *pianissimo* and very delicate. Easy enough to understand but hard to play! Keep the movement in 3 beats per measure (not 6), sweeping through the opening gesture which interlocks the hands and then crosses them (a solution Debussy himself suggests by writing it out in m. 75 and similar), and continuing that momentum through the second and third beats; the movement must feel swept in general, as the *andantino* marking and triple meter suggest. There is no real place for the *tempo rubato* we find in the "Prélude," for example.

m. 5: Be careful to observe the *pianissimo*! Also, careful attention to voicing the top of the thirds will enhance the beauty of this passage, as well as a recognition of the metric *hemiola* written out over the next four measures. It feels that Debussy has shifted the meter from 3 to 4 here, and one must phrase accordingly. The technique needed for the thirds depends on using the hands as a unit (not playing only from the fingers), lifting the wrist on the downbeat and then "tucking in" the thirty-second notes before falling again with the wrist on the "and" of the first beat. The same holds true for beat 3 of this measure and the analogous places in measures 6 and 7, although in those last two measures feel free to release the quarter notes being played by the thumb on beats 2, 3 and 1 respectively.

mm. 10–11: It is helpful to think of these two measures as one big unit, with measure 11 resolving harmonically and gradually hushing into the **pp** of measure 12.

mm. 12–14: Some of the trickiest and most awkward passages in the entire suite. One has to throw the right to the chord on the "and" of the first beat, lifting from the wrist on the second beat so as to be ready to "tuck in" the grace notes before dropping the hand again on the "and" of the second beat, in each measure. It requires careful coordination. Another piece of advice would be to practice the upper two voices separately (the off-beat thirds), to develop a feeling of security in those weaker fingers. The knuckles should be firm, again treating the hand as a unit (not playing from the fingers alone). Observe that measure 14 need not be *legato* at any point.

mm. 19–21: The *sforzandos* in these measures ought to be played within the **p** dynamic. Note, too, the final "sideways" accent in measure 21, which should be played differently than the *staccatos* which conclude measures 19 and 20.

m. 22: The tiniest releases of the left-hand slurs are appropriate here.

m. 23: Be sure to follow the *diminuendo* faithfully without bumping the second beat, despite the leap in both hands. The soprano D on beat 2 ought to sing audibly above the alto line, the same idea also being found in measure 25 and following.

mm. 26: Now *espressivo*! Feel emotion strengthening like the incoming tide, especially from measure 30, achieving a climactic break on the beach (but only *forte*!) at measure 35. Shed emotional backwash by measure 38.

mm. 27 and 29: Be careful not to stop the phrase on the downbeat; the F continues on to the G on the "and" of the second beat in each measure, which should not be bumped.

mm. 33–34: Be sure to hold the pedal through both measures; I recommend the same for measures 35–36, to keep the continuity of the bass.

mm. 37: Note the F in the left-hand chord on beat 2 (different from m. 35).

mm. 38 and 40: The right hand must throw from register to register with the most *legato* motion possible.

m. 43: Note the *legato*.

m. 58: As in measure 22, the slurs ought to be gently released, with attention also to correct metric accents (less on beat 2).

mm. 60–61: It is a very beautiful effect to *crescendo* in the melody to the downbeat of measure 61, but *decrescendo* all other voices. This honors Debussy's intent while coloring it in a truly sensitive way.
m. 64: It is possibly not worth it to do the fingering redistributions I have suggested here, but I find it better for shaping the melodic contour, which must be released gently at the conclusion of the phrase despite the *crescendo*.

m. 67: Be careful to tie the right-hand B on the third beat over to the next measure.

m. 73: I interpret the right-hand accent on beat 2 and the following *tenuto* on beat 3 to be for the top voice only (also in m. 74). The left hand of course should respect its *tenutos*.

m. 76: This rhythm is really pernicious since there have been grace notes up to this point. Playing it exactly in time seems rather dogmatic, so I do treat it with "grace-note" abandon—taking care however to place it exactly upon the second sixteenth beat.

mm. 78–79: Using the right-hand fifth finger on the last note of each measure, you can use it and the wrist to pivot to the hand position that begins the next measure (thus preparing the thumb for the downbeat as well).

m. 82: The *très soutenu* (very sustained) nature of this phrase would seem to indicate a return to the expressive nature of its previous appearance (m. 26 and following). Use the pedal to sustain the grace note E in the bass throughout the measure, which seems expected by Debussy since he gives a quarter rest in the bass on the downbeat of measure 83.

m. 86: A temptation would be to make a singing melody out of the left-hand thumb, but really the melody must sing out from the soprano since that is the only consistent voice all the way until measure 97. Be careful to shape the left-hand gestures well, and not "vertically" (but observe the *tenutos* in m. 89).

m. 87: Many previous editions give F-naturals instead of F-sharps; I, however, am convinced by Roy Howat's argument for the present reading, as articulated in the Durand critical edition.

m. 93: The left hand should be accomplished in one sweeping gesture, not vertically (also in m. 95); but note the reversed dynamic indications! The difference in left-hand rhythm and accentuation is also carefully marked between measure 94 (dotted half-note) and measure 96 (a released quarter note, although no pedal change is necessary). Right hand: Cultivate a very firm fifth finger, supported by a firm knuckle and a free arm, to bring out this melody. Note also the tie into measure 95, which means that the last soprano note of measure 94 must be played with appropriate strength.

m. 102: The *glissando* can be accomplished using the right-hand third and fourth fingers together, twisting neatly at the very top to get a clear (but ***ppp***) final note with the third finger. Every note should be clear to the very top!

Clair de lune: Andante très expressif

Surely the most well-known and arguably the best-loved of Debussy's *oeuvre*, "Clair de lune" ("Moonlight") is a special piece unto its own, despite its appearance as the third movement of the *Suite bergamasque*. The "very expressive" Andante, indicated from the outset as the character for the entire movement, requests a slow tempo and voluptuous phrasing. The best performances of "Clair de lune" are patient, loving, and attentive above all to beauty of sound and flow of rhythm. The music should enchant us, not stir us emotionally. As a piece of musical magic, it stands with any movement of any piece in all of Debussy's output.

m. 1–14: Note that the movement beings with a rest, which must be felt if the rhythm of the first gesture is to be executed well; subdividing the triplets internally from the very beginning is part of the secret to making *rubatos* organic in the first 14 measures or so—not so as to be metronomically inflexible, but rather to feel time organically and fluidly, yet still tied to three triplets (of whatever value) per pulse. This will be important as you feel the resistance to the inner pulse in measures that include duplets (mm. 3, 13, etc.). Voicing must be carefully sculpted throughout, with a very beautiful *legato* in as many voices as possible through finger substitution.

m. 1: Be sure to feel the distance from the left-hand A-flat to the right-hand A-flat—the expression is in the reaching. *Con sordina* (with mute) means, in this case, "with *una corda.*"

m. 9: Take your time through the triplet to hear the colors of each register and feel the distance between them.

m. 10 and similar: Be careful not to accent the chords which appear on off beats; technically and musically they should be released from the long notes which precede them.

m. 11 and following: Hold the pedal through the entire measure, because of the dotted half note in the bass. Additionally, the last notes of each measure in the right hand should be held as you change the pedal for the following downbeat.

m. 15 and following: "*Rubato*" is an Italian term that originates in the word "*rubare,*" which means "to steal." Stealing means that you don't give back. My understanding of this *tempo rubato* is to steal time and then return to tempo as if nothing ever happened. This works both ways: one could flow faster or slower, but proportions need not be mathematically evened out. What ought to be observed more carefully, in fact, is the *tenuto* articulations, for example in measure 15. Be fairly even and equal when they are present; when they are not present (i.e. m. 17), be free. Therefore, on the downbeat of measure 15, I prefer to "feel" the E-flat octave rather than to plant it, to let the sound float up from that register to the magical chord on the second half of that beat—but outside of any tempo. It recalls the opening reach of the piece.

m. 18: The grace note is melodic and should not be played too fast. Be sure to hold the last chord in the right hand as you change pedal for measure 19.

m. 19 and similar: Be sure to voice the melody in the right hand and left hand with softer chords inside, and a fluid shape. The *crescendo* can be graded over the next few measures by listening to the ascent of the bass line (listening to harmonic resolutions along the way), and then the *diminuendo* shaped by its fall in measures 25 and 26. Throughout, pay close attention to the presence of *tenutos* (or lack thereof)—they will have an effect on the "*animé*" (animation) and how we grade that as well.

mm. 25–26: The rolled chords should be expressive and varied in tempo, not just ripped off in one speed. Personally, I don't mind a continuous roll from bottom to top, as opposed to the traditional execution of broken rolls when notated this way (each hand rolled independently).

m. 27: "*Un poco mosso*" means "a little moving," it is true—but not too much faster! Already there is contrast to the slowing tempo of the previous measures, by virtue of the rolling arpeggios.

mm. 27–29: Be careful to observe the phrasing of each measure, which should *diminuendo* and release in the right hand (except in the presence of a *crescendo*, as in m. 29). The accompanimental arpeggios in these measures, although broken between the hands, should be carefully shaped to taper away at the end of each slur, with gentle emphasis on the bass notes as you change color with each new harmony. The left hand should not feel obliged to *crescendo* in tandem with the right hand in measure 29; rather, all of measures 29 and 30 should feel like the slow cresting of a particularly warm and caressing wave of water.

m. 30: I would encourage the thumb of the left hand to pretend it is a French horn when the melodic echo starts on the second beat; a rather bronzed sound, hollow but *maestoso*, not too forceful and a little distant (but "present" at the same time). The right hand should continue with this sound. The orchestration of the right hand starting in measure 29 is left to the discretion of the performer.

m. 32: Be sure to observe the *subito piano*; this is a very typical dynamic occurrence in Debussy's music.

m. 33: The wrist of the right hand can use the sixteenth notes to gently circle around to the next melody notes.

m. 37: It is at this point that you should start to release the *una corda*, which should have been depressed up to this moment from the start of the piece (with a possible hiatus in mm. 21-25). Be sure to release the last sixteenth note of each right-hand group in preparation for the next gesture. Since Debussy indicates "*En animant*" (becoming animated), let the *più crescendo* occur naturally from the gentle quickening that will occur. Neither *crescendo* nor *accelerando* need be much, since Debussy takes care of the increased animation through shorter slurs.

mm. 43–50: The "*calmato*" can refer also to sound, not just tempo. Resume coloring with the *una corda* at measure 43 (perhaps not fully depressed yet); and I suggest that we plan to save most of the *rallentando* for measures 49 and 50.

m. 43: When throwing the right hand to the chord on beat 3, take care to resolve the melody in the thumb and hold it all the way through to the end of the measure; also in measure 44. Measures 45–46 present similar challenges in the right hand from beat 3 in each measure; the left hand addresses these challenges in measures 47 and 48.

mm. 51–end: This concluding section must feel airy and timeless, although for the performer it will be essential to subdivide as at the beginning of the piece.

m. 51 and similar: The *tenuto* on the third beat should be well placed and played softly in order to conserve the feeling of a "third beat," not an "equal pulse" within the measure.

m. 53: Please note the difference between the right hand second beat of this measure and that of measure 3.

m 55: The right-hand fingering for the final beat of the measure is best executed if one delays the finger substitution in the alto (1 to 2) voice until after the soprano has been played with the fourth finger.

m. 65: Treat the duple in the left hand very lightly; the melody note on beat 2 is the F in the right hand. The left hand A-flat which crosses the right hand at that moment simply shines as a color.

m. 66: "*morendo jusqu'à la fin*"—"dying away until the end."

m. 71: As you move from sixteenths to eighth notes, be careful to effect a smooth transition, without bumps.

Passepied: Allegretto ma non troppo

As mentioned above, most passepieds are in a light 3, instead of the duple time signature marked by Debussy. In fact, the original was in 4/4, but new research by Roy Howat argues that the character and tempo seem to demand a "cut-time" feeling.

mm. 1 and following: Make a very slight difference in sound between the bass line and the rest of the *staccatos*. It might be enough to merely "think" it. But all the *staccatos* in the left hand must be listened to for consistent sound and short release.

m. 5: Although there is a difference in expression between the *staccato* articulation of the melody (in the preceding measure) and the *legato* found here, this should not be exaggerated.

mm. 8 and similar: Be sure to release the thumb and not to bang it on the downbeat.

m. 9: This left-hand fingering is very useful for the many similar places in this movement, with very few exceptions. It rolls the hand gently, encouraging relaxation by keeping the hand collected in a natural span (and therefore allowing better finger articulation), and you can throw gently back to the fifth finger for the next figure.

m. 11: Note the difference in the left hand between this measure and measure 114.

mm. 15 and similar: The two-note slurs can be accomplished with a down-up motion of the wrist, as usual, pivoting slightly on the second finger. A tiny amount of connective pedal between the two chords, released as the wrist is released, would also be helpful, but not necessary if it overwhelms the sound or texture.

mm. 27 and following: Be sure to shape the bass line.

m. 30: The melody is in the right-hand thumb, and should be voiced accordingly. The left-hand fingering for the second half of the measure is one of the few exceptions to the fingering rule outlined in the note to m. 9. Still collect the hand and throw the fifth finger back down to the downbeat of m. 31, but without the second finger crossing the thumb as at other times.

mm. 39 and similar: The stretch in the left hand on the fourth beat is awkward; it may be helpful to aim for the second finger, allowing the third finger to fall with it.

mm. 40 and similar: The right hand can quickly release the chord and the thumb underneath the melody notes, although these should not be truly *staccato*.

m. 43: "*Cédez un peu*"—"slowing a little"; both here and in m. 80, this ought to be understood as a natural release of momentum, as if a spinning wheel is let go to gradually decelerate, without applying a brake. In this way you can make a difference between "*Cédez*" and "*ritardando*," which is a more determined slowing (with brakes). Since the *cédez* in m. 43 is comparatively brief, however, it is simply a gentle and hesitant pulling back, a moment perhaps of deeper expression: you don't need to make too much of it

mm. 43 and following: Note the very long slurs which indicate extended phrases; be careful not to bump any chords, creating false accents in the melodic line, which should sing out.

mm. 51 and following: Take care to delicately shape the bass line, but not at the expense of the melody, which must be the strongest sound, even in its decay.

mm. 59 and following: Careful attention to voicing and the three different kinds of articulation are called for here. The repeated chords can easily be produced by a gentle ricochet from a dropped wrist, playing from the hand as a unit, and not thinking "only fingers." The fingers, however, should be very light and articulate to produce the *staccatos*.

m. 67: Again, shape the bass line.

mm. 74–75: Be careful to pass the phrase from left hand to right hand so there is no bump or break.

m. 80: *Cédez*…see note to measure 43.

m. 83: I find no satisfactory solution here, in terms of a smooth *legato* in the bass, combined with an *a tempo* transition to the next measure, all the while keeping the integrity (primacy) of the melody. One wishes that Debussy had started this *a tempo* a measure later, somehow.

mm. 88 and following: Some slight pedal on the *tenutos* could be welcome, and you will end up holding the pedal through m. 91 in order not to lose the whole-note chord in the right hand. Continue the *staccato* in the left hand, however, despite the pedal.

mm. 95 and following: Be sure to shape the gestures that pass between hands without bumps.

m. 104: There is a temptation to keep the pedal from the preceding measures without changing, but it ought to be changed here, to help the *diminuendo*. In Debussy's mind, this *diminuendo* probably implies a tiny *cédez*, because of the *premier tempo* that he marks in m. 106. This *premier tempo* indicates not just a return to the first tempo (if you have left it…), but also a return to the opening character of the piece.

mm. 106–109: Tiny cotton-ball touches of pedal to help each of the long notes would be very appropriate here, and then back to a drier *staccato* in m. 110.
m. 114: See note to m. 11.

mm. 125 and following: Although Debussy does not suggest a melodic shape through writing a slur, you can shape a long line with good attention to absolutely even triplets (over a running and very quiet LH) and broad, albeit quiet, sound. Tiny amounts of pedal will be valuable, until you go for a more beautiful wash in measure 128.

mm. 132–138: I can't resist holding the pedal from the bass E on the downbeat of m. 132 for a long time, gradually "feathering out" the pedal as I approach m. 138. Be careful not to create false accents with the entrance of the left hand in measures 134–137, although it does create an interesting rhythm if not overdone.

m. 138: See note to m. 39.

m. 142: Note the *staccatos*. It doesn't mean that you should not use pedal; it just allows us more expressive possibility on the first two notes of the phrase.

m. 143: The arpeggio that begins in the left hand ought to be full of color, but never swamping the decay of the melody C-sharp. Even as it continues in measure 144, it ought to get brighter, but also softer.

m. 147: The right hand is accompanimental and "color" now; the left hand has the melody in augmented form, and should be brought out in as *legato* a shape as possible. The right-hand chord on the downbeat of measure 147 should be heard to resolve from the right-hand diad on the downbeat of measure 145; it continues to shimmer like stars, requiring articulate finger tips despite the use of the *una corda*—but *legato* as well!

m. 152: Don't give in to the temptation to use the right hand when the left hand clef changes to treble—the right hand should continue to sing through the whole-note chord.

m. 154 to the end: Tiny touches of pedal are appropriate here, with careful attention to voicing.

References

Dumesnil, Maurice. *How to Play and Teach Debussy*. New York: Schroeder and Gunther, Inc., 1932.

Howat, Roy. *The Art of French Piano Music*. New Haven and London: Yale University Press, 2009.

Long, Marguerite. *At the Piano with Debussy*, trl. Olive Senior-Ellis. London: J.M. Dent and Sons Ltd., 1972.

Raad, Virginia. *The Piano Sonority of Claude Debussy*. Lewiston/Queenston/Lampeter: The Edwin Mellen Press, 1994.

Schmitz, E. Robert. *The Piano Works of Claude Debussy*. New York: Dover Publications, Inc., 1966.

Acknowledgement

I am greatly indebted to Karen Taylor for her unstinting and untiring helpfulness in searching out answers to obscure technical questions. Her passion for French music and pianists, and her devotion to her friends, are a great inspiration to the many lives she has touched with her superb musicianship and teaching.

Audio Credits

David Lau, Recording Engineer, Brookwood Studios

Eun Young Lee and Yoonji Seo, Recording Assistants

Steinway Piano

Suite bergamasque
Prélude

Claude Debussy

Moderato (tempo rubato) [♩ = 104]

Menuet

Clair de lune

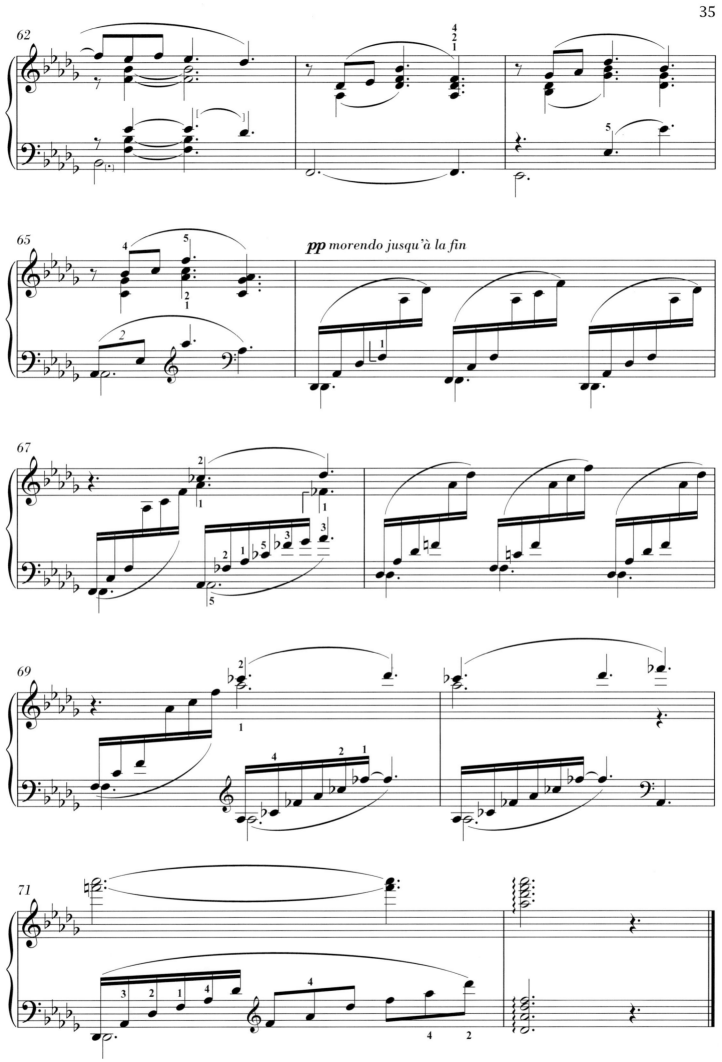

pp morendo jusqu'à la fin

Passepied

1° Tempo

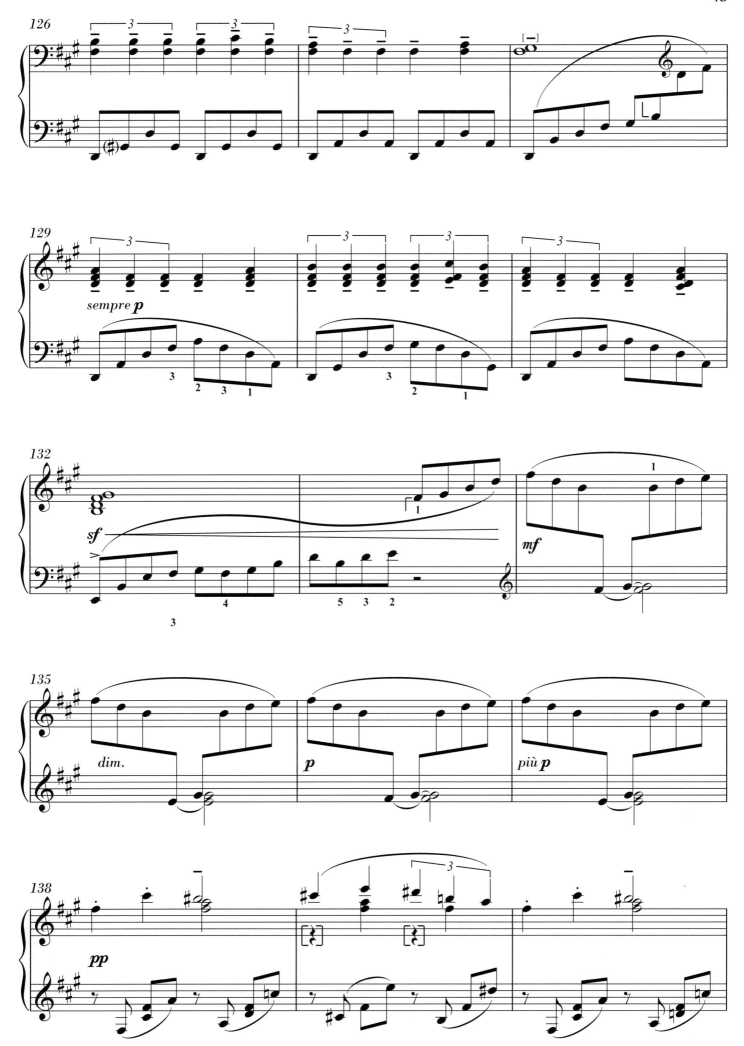

ABOUT THE EDITOR

CHRISTOPHER HARDING

Pianist **Christopher Harding** maintains a flourishing international performance career, generating acclaim and impressing audiences and critics alike with his substantive interpretations and pianistic mastery. He has given frequent solo, concerto, and chamber music performances in venues as far flung as the Kennedy Center and Phillips Collection in Washington, D.C., Suntory Hall in Tokyo and the National Theater Concert Hall in Taipei, the Jack Singer Concert Hall in Calgary, and halls and festival appearances in Newfoundland, Israel, Romania, and China. His concerto performances have included concerts with the National Symphony and the Saint Louis Symphony Orchestras, the San Angelo and Santa Barbara Symphonies, and the Tokyo City Philharmonic, working with such conductors as Andrew Sewell, Eric Zhou, Taijiro Iimori, Gisele Ben-Dor, Fabio Machetti, Randall Craig Fleisher, John DeMain, Ron Spiegelman, Daniel Alcott, and Darryl One, among others. His chamber music and duo collaborations have included internationally renowned artists such as clarinetist Karl Leister, flautist András Adorján, and members of the St. Lawrence and Ying String Quartets, in addition to frequent projects with his distinguished faculty colleagues at the University of Michigan. He has recorded solo and chamber music CDs for the Equilibrium and Brevard Classics labels. He has additionally edited and published critical editions and recordings of works by Claude Debussy (*Children's Corner*, Arabesques and shorter works) and Wolfgang Amadeus Mozart (Viennese Sonatinas) for the Schirmer Performance Editions published by Hal Leonard.

Professor Harding is Chair of Piano and Associate Professor of Piano Performance and Chamber Music at the University of Michigan School of Music, Theatre and Dance. He has presented master classes and lecture recitals in universities across the United States and Asia, as well as in Israel and Canada. His most recent tours to Taiwan, Hong Kong, and mainland China included presentations and master classes at Hong Kong Baptist University, National Taiwan Normal University, SooChow University, the National Taiwan University of Education, and conservatories and universities in Beijing (Central and China Conservatories), Tianjin, Shanghai, Hefei, Guangzhou, Shenyang, Dalien, and Chongqing. He has additionally performed and lectured numerous times in Seoul, including lecture recitals and classes at Seoul National University, Ewha Women's University, and Dong Duk University. He has served in extended tours as a Fulbright Senior Specialist at the Sichuan Conservatory of Music in Chengdu, China (2008), and also at Seoul National University (2011). While teaching at SNU, he simultaneously held a Special Chair in Piano at Ewha Womans' University.

In addition to teaching undergraduate and graduate piano performance and chamber music at the University of Michigan School of Music, Theatre and Dance, Mr. Harding also serves on the faculty of the Indiana University Summer Piano Academy and is a frequent guest artist and teacher at the MasterWorks Festival in Winona Lake, IN. Recent summer festivals have also included the Chautauqua Institution in New York, and the Rebecca Penneys Piano Festival in Tampa, Florida.

Mr. Harding was born of American parents in Munich, Germany and raised in Northern Virginia. His collegiate studies were with Menahem Pressler and Nelita True. Prior to college, he worked for ten years with Milton Kidd at the American University Department of Performing Arts Preparatory Division, where he was trained in the traditions of Tobias Matthay. He has taken twenty-five first prizes in national and international competitions and in 1999 was awarded the special "Mozart Prize" at the Cleveland International Piano Competition, given for the best performance of a composition by Mozart.